Cambridge Young Learners English Tests

Cambridge Flyers 3

Examination papers from

University of Cambridge
ESOL Examinations:

English for Speakers of Other Languages

CAMBRIDGE
UNIVERSITY PRESS

CAMBRIDGE UNIVERSITY PRESS
Cambridge, New York, Melbourne, Madrid, Cape Town, Singapore, São Paulo

Cambridge University Press
The Edinburgh Building, Cambridge CB2 2RU, UK

www.cambridge.org
Information on this title: www.cambridge.org/9780521755245

First published 2003
6th printing 2006

Printed in the United Kingdom at the University Press, Cambridge

A catalogue record for this publication is available from the British Library

ISBN-13 978-0-521-75524-5 Student's Book
ISBN-10 0-521-75524-7 Student's Book

ISBN-13 978-0-521-75525-2 Answer Booklet
ISBN-10 0-521-75525-5 Answer Booklet

ISBN-13 978-0-521-75526-9 Cassette
ISBN-10 0-521-75526-3 Cassette

Contents

Test 1
Listening

Part 1
– 5 questions –

Listen and draw lines. There is one example.

Emma

Harry

Helen

Richard

Nick

William

Betty

Part 2
– 5 questions –

Listen and write. There is one example.

KATY'S HOLIDAYS

	Needs new:	*clothes*
	Holiday:	
1	Where?	....
2	Get there:	....
3	Who with?	....
4	Sports:	Swimming and ....
5	Homework:	....

Part 3
– 5 questions –

Where did David leave his things?

Listen and write letters in the boxes. There is one example.

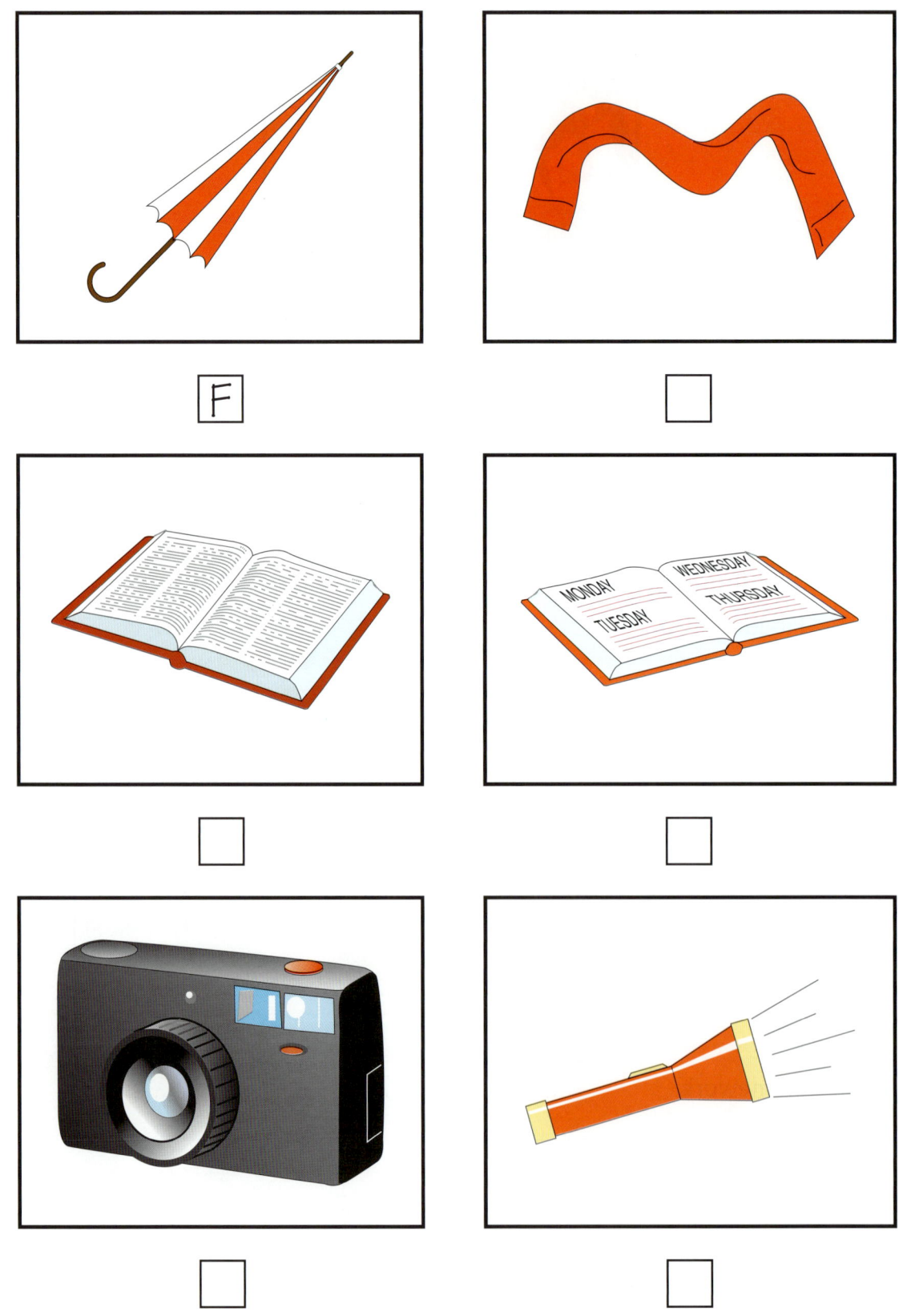

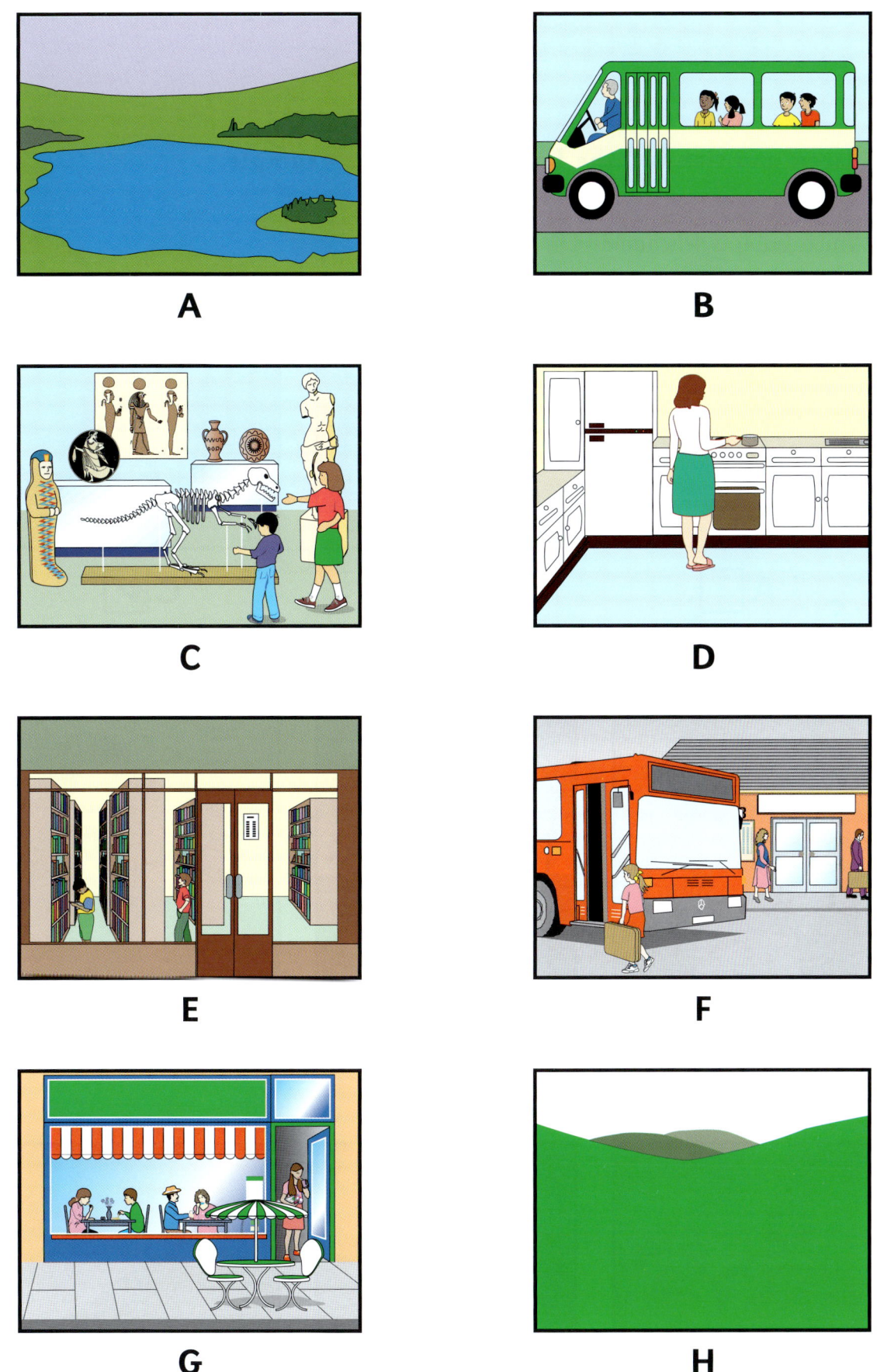

A

B

C

D

E

F

G

H

Part 4
– 5 questions –

Listen and tick (✔) the box. There is one example.

Which baby is Michael?

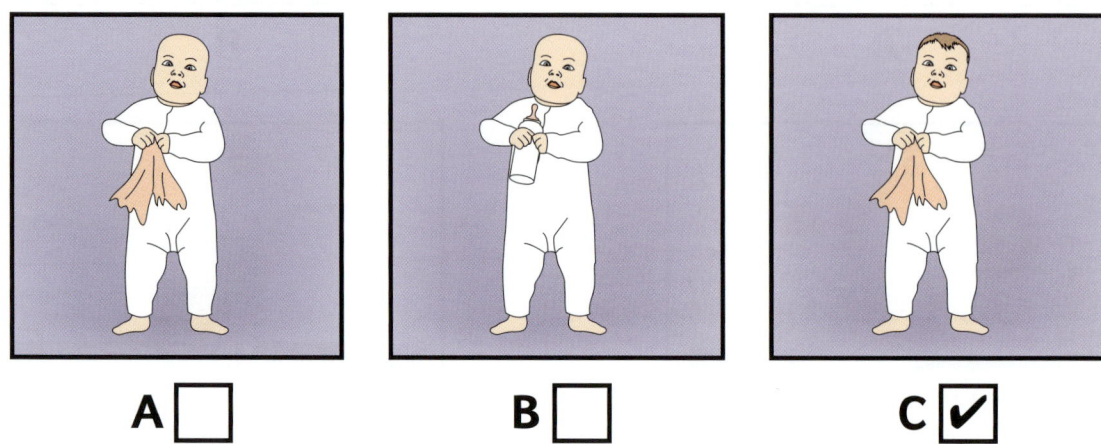

A ☐   B ☐   C ✔

1   Which is Michael's grandfather?

A ☐   B ☐   C ☐

2   Where did Michael's family live?

A ☐   B ☐   C ☐

3   Where did Michael's family go on holiday?

A ☐   B ☐   C ☐

4   Which photo are they talking about?

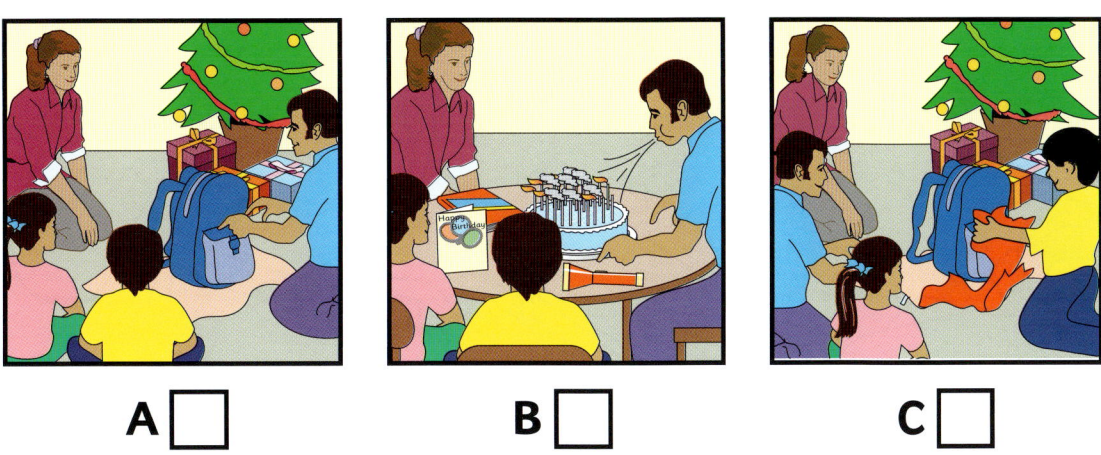

A ☐   B ☐   C ☐

5   Which boy is Michael?

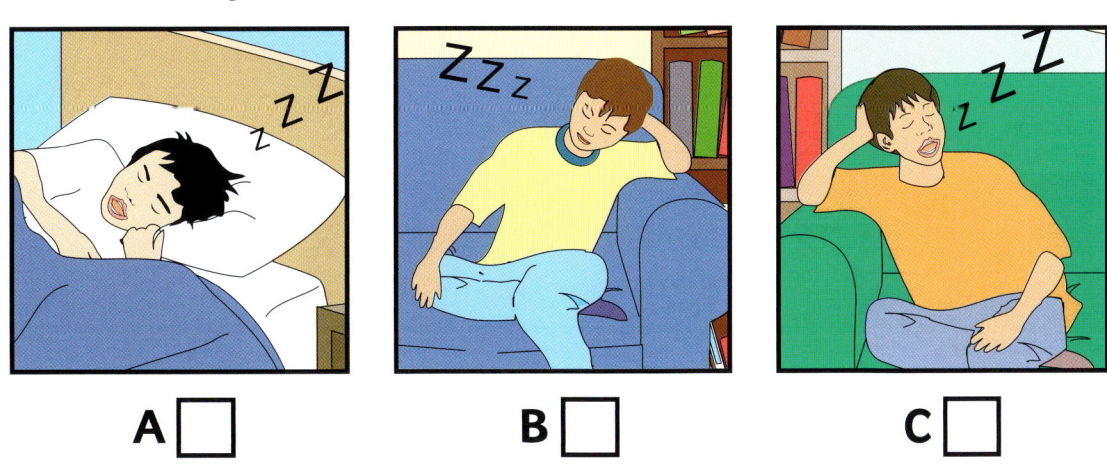

A ☐   B ☐   C ☐

Part 5
– 5 questions –

Listen and colour and draw and write. There is one example.

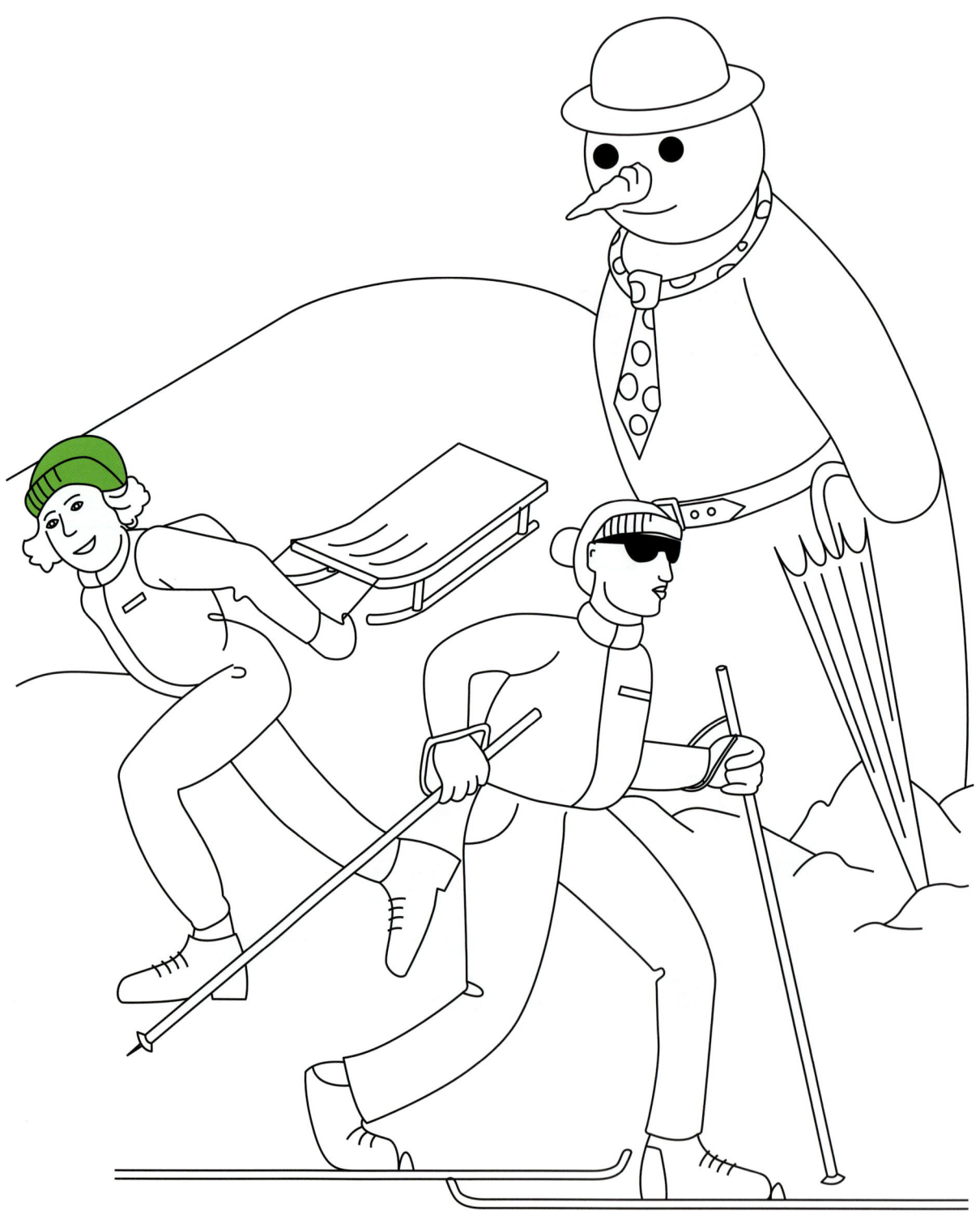

Reading and Writing

Part 1

– 10 questions –

Look and read. Choose the correct words and write them on the lines. There is one example.

a university   journalists   a dictionary   an actor

scissors

a dentist

a knife

jam

This is made of different kinds of fruit, and you can eat it with bread and butter. ....*jam*..........

1   You can make this with a lot of different vegetables, but you don't cook it.   ....

2   This is someone who works in the theatre, in films or on TV.   ....

3   You use these for cutting paper and card. You can cut your hair with them too. ....

4   This has a kind of bread at the bottom, with cheese and tomatoes on top of it, and you cook it.   ....

5   You go to this person when you have toothache, and he or she helps you.   ....

6   This is white or brown and you use it when you make cakes, biscuits and pasta.   ....

7   This is something that you study at school, for example, English, History or Science.   ....

8   These people write for newspapers or magazines. They also work for TV or radio.   ....

9   If you can't spell a word, you might look for it in this book.   ....

10 These people fly planes to all parts of the world.   ....

a salad

flour

pilots

rice

a subject   a pizza   a cook

11

Part 2
– 7 questions –

Look and read. Write yes or no.

Examples

There is an old, grey castle on the highest hill.   .....*yes*.....

Three swans are flying over the lake.   .....*no*.....

Questions

1   The crocodile is too tall to get
     into the cave.   ....

2   One of the dogs is walking up
     the hill through the trees.   ....

3   The bear is looking at the clock
     on the castle wall.   ....

4   Most of the flags have got an
     orange square on them.   ....

5   The girl with blonde hair has
     drawn a picture of two butterflies.   ....

6   The queen is riding a dark brown
     horse with a long neck.   ....

7   The man is throwing a ball into
     the water.   ....

Part 3
– 5 questions –

Read the text and choose the best answer.

Example

Sue: Hello, Michael.

Michael: (A)   Hello, Sue.

                        B   Bye-bye.

                        C   That's nice.

Questions

1   **Sue:**   Where was your sister today? She didn't come
                        to school.

    Michael: A   No, I went shopping.

                                B   No, you weren't there.

                                C   No, she had to stay
                                        in bed.

2 **Sue:** Oh! Is she ill?

 Michael: A Yes, she's got a cold.

 B Yes, she's fine now.

 C Yes, she's right.

3 **Sue:** Will she be at school tomorrow, then?

 Michael: A She has been.

 B She might be.

 C She was there.

4 **Sue:** We've got a Maths test tomorrow morning.
 Can you tell her?

 Michael: A Yes, there is.

 B All right, we did.

 C OK, I will.

5 **Sue:** I must go now. I've got a lot of homework
 to do tonight.

 Michael: A Thank you.

 B Excuse me.

 C OK. Bye, then.

Part 4
– 6 questions –

Read the story. Look at the pictures and the two examples. Write one-word answers.

My name is Nick. I live with my mum and dad and our ....cat............

Bill. Last weekend we moved to a new house, so I helped my mum and

dad. I ....carried......... my toys out to the car. Some men came and

took the sofa, chairs, armchairs, tables and beds to our new house. The

sofa was very .... so it was difficult to move. We left at

12 o'clock, and later in the afternoon we arrived at our new home. It was

much bigger than our old house, with a long garden. The men took the

beds to our new bedrooms, and we put the books and toys on

the .... In the evening, we were ....

our supper when Dad asked, 'Where's Bill?' We ....

everywhere, but we couldn't find him. 'Oh, no!' said Mum. 'I think we've

left him at our old house!' When we got to the house, Bill was waiting in

the garden. He was very .... to see us. 'Sorry, Bill!' I said.

What's the best name for this story?

Tick one box.

Bill wants a new home ☐

Bill leaves his family ☐

Bill has to wait ☐

Part 5
– 7 questions –

Look at the pictures and read the story. Answer the questions. Do not write more than four words in each answer.

Emma loved writing. Every day, when she got home from school, she wrote in her diary. She wrote about everyone at school. After school, Emma's friends always said, "Come and play with us. We're going to the park." "No," said Emma. "I can't. I've got to do my homework." But she didn't do her homework, she wrote in her diary. At school, when they saw her diary, they asked her, "What do you write about?" "It's a secret!" she answered, and put it in her bag.

Example

What did Emma write in every day?   *her diary*
....

Questions

1   Who did she write about?   ....

2   Where did Emma's friends play after school?   ....

3   Where did Emma put her diary when she
    was at school?   ....

Then one day, Emma saw her sister Helen with her friend Katy. She followed them to the park and listened to them carefully. She could hear everything that they said, but they couldn't see her. It wasn't very interesting, but Emma wrote about it. The next day, Emma left the diary in the classroom when she went home.

4   Who was with Katy?   ....

5   What did Emma leave at school?   ....

Katy found the diary and started to read it. She was very unhappy, so she took it to Emma's house. "I found your diary," she said. "You shouldn't follow people and write about them!" "I'm sorry," said Emma, "but read the next page." Katy read it. It said, 'April 6th – I like Katy very much. She's my best friend!' "OK, Emma!" said Katy. "But don't follow me again, please!" "I'll only write about school," Emma said. "And I won't follow you again!"

6   How did Katy feel when she
     read the diary?   ....

7   When did Emma write about
     her best friend?   ....

Blank Page

Part 6
– 10 questions –

Read the text. Choose the right words and write them on the lines.

PAPER

Example Most paper is made from wood, but you ....*can*.................

make it from other kinds of plants and leaves too. People made

1 .... first paper about two thousand years ago.

2 At the time, it .... very expensive because it was

3 made by hand, ... now it is much cheaper.

4 We use paper for .... different things, like writing,

reading and drawing. Postcards, cards, envelopes and books

5 .... all made of paper. We also use paper to make

kites, fans, and the cups that we take on picnics. When we go

6 shopping, we carry things .... paper bags. At school

7 we .... on paper. In art classes we make things from

it – we cut it, colour it and glue it. Now you can also buy clothes

8 made of paper, and when they get dirty, you put ....

9 in the bin! We have .... use a lot of trees to make

10 paper. We shouldn't use too much of it .... we

don't want to lose all our trees.

Example	can	will	must
1	a	the	an
2	was	is	be
3	if	when	but
4	much	many	more
5	were	are	being
6	on	over	in
7	writing	write	writes
8	them	they	their
9	at	for	to
10	because	so	than

Part 7
– 5 questions –

Read the letter and write the missing words. Write one word on each line.

Dear Ben,

Example Last weekend, Tom, William and I ....**went**............ camping in

1 Tom's garden. It was a dark .... on Saturday, and

we couldn't see the moon or the stars. After supper, we went

2 .... the tent. We were laughing and

3 .... songs when we heard something outside. Tom

4 said, "It's .... animal." "It might be a bear," said

William. We were afraid, but when Tom went outside, it

5 .... only his dad. "I've brought you some hot

chocolate," he said.

See you soon!

love from Richard

Blank Page

Listening

Part 1
– 5 questions –

Listen and draw lines. There is one example.

Sarah   William   Richard

Michael   Emma   David   Helen

Part 2
– 5 questions –

Listen and write. There is one example.

A FAMOUS ACTRESS

	Name:	Betty .... Fountain ....
1	How old?	....
2	Food:	Salad, ... and fish
	Homes:	flat in city
3		house in a ....
	Holidays:	winter – skiing
4		summer – ....
5		with her ....

Part 3
– 5 questions –

Where did William's aunt take each photo?

Listen and write letters in the boxes. There is one example.

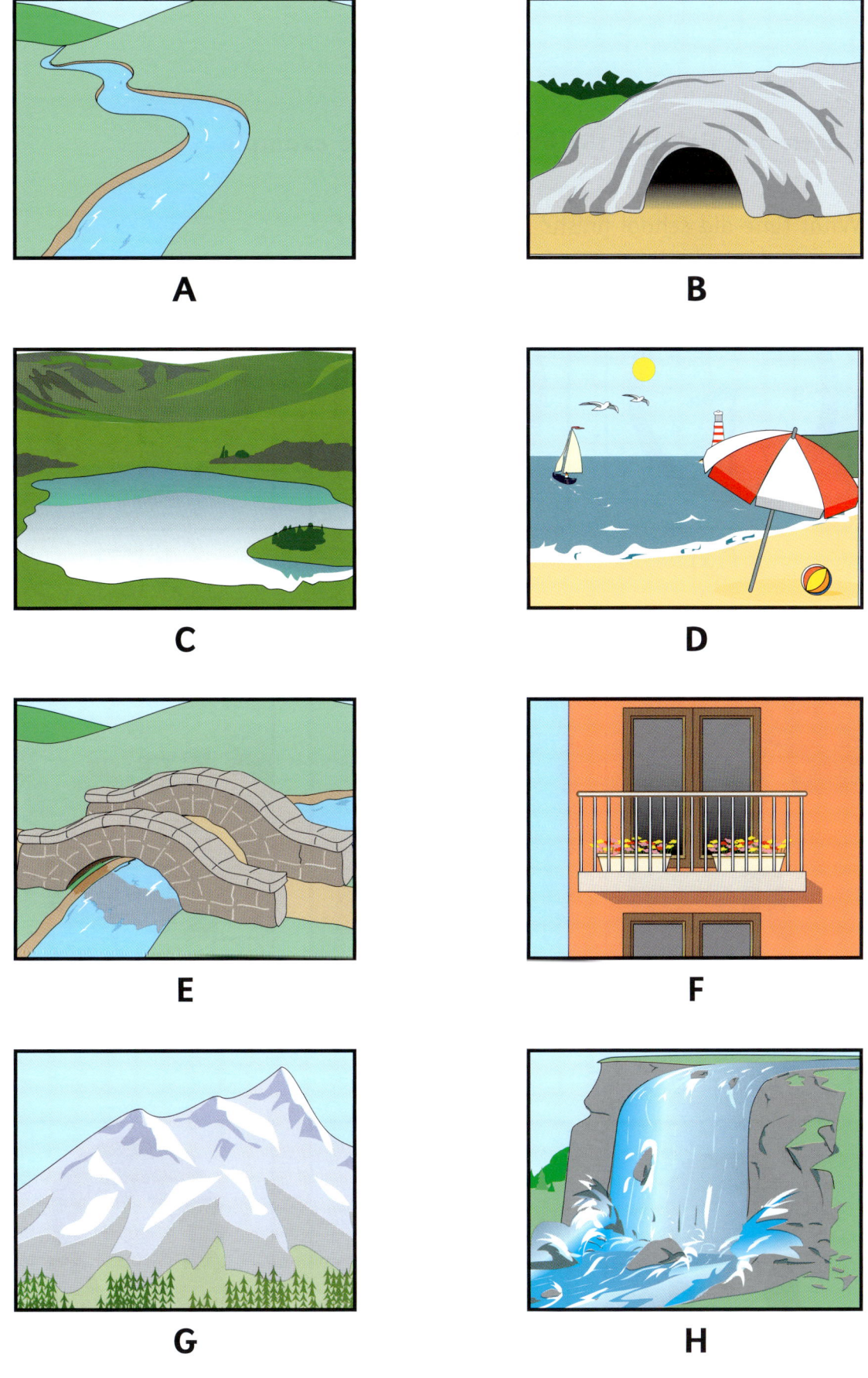

A

B

C

D

E

F

G

H

Part 4
– 5 questions –

Listen and tick (✔) the box. There is one example.

What time did school finish?

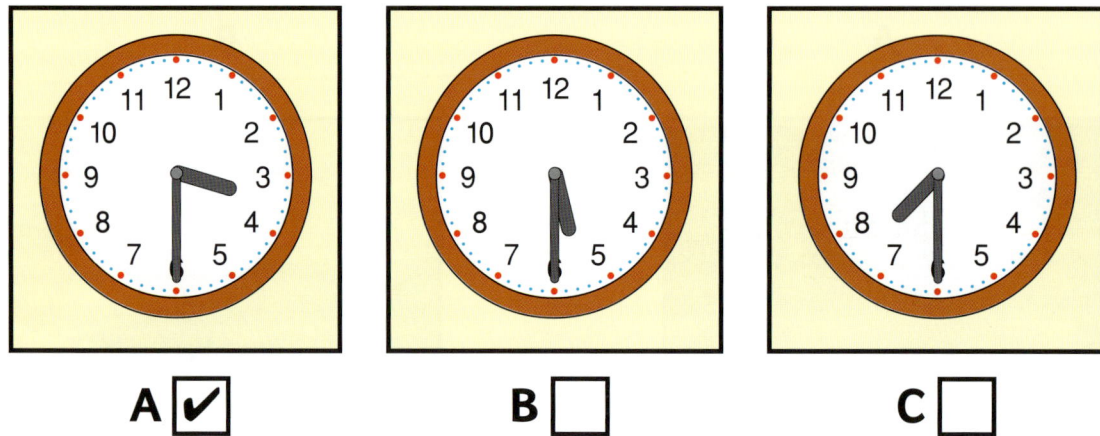

A ✔ B ☐ C ☐

1 Which is Sarah's favourite lesson?

A ☐ B ☐ C ☐

2 Which girl is Sally?

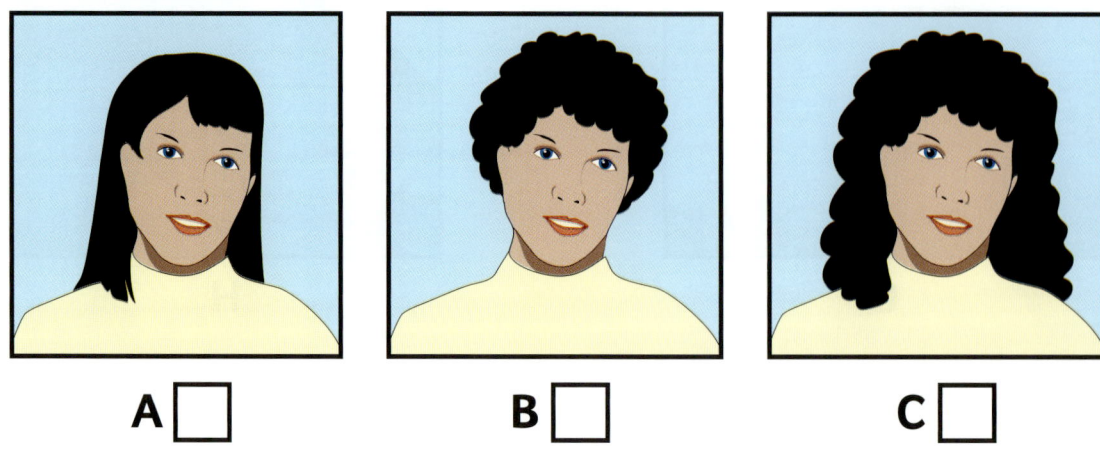

A ☐ B ☐ C ☐

3   Which team is Sarah in?

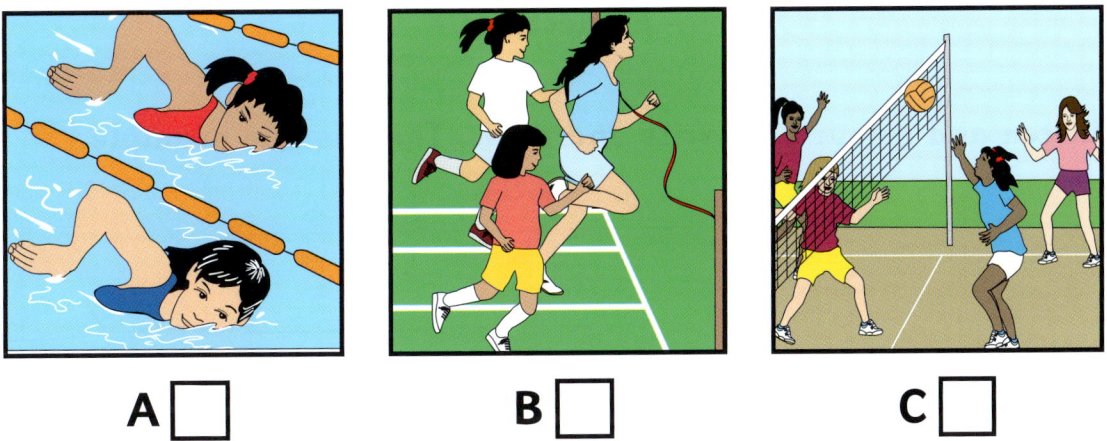

A ☐   B ☐   C ☐

4   What did Sarah have for lunch?

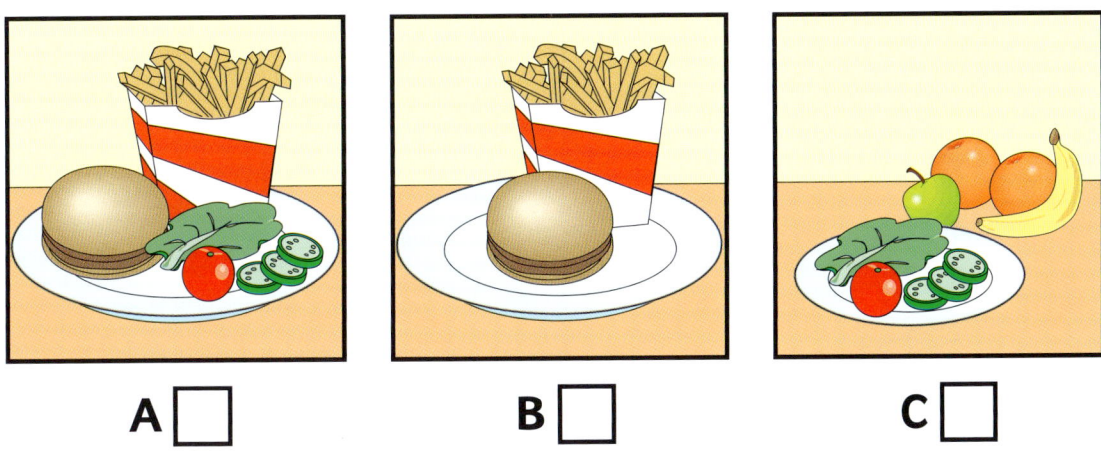

A ☐   B ☐   C ☐

5   What is Sarah going to do next?

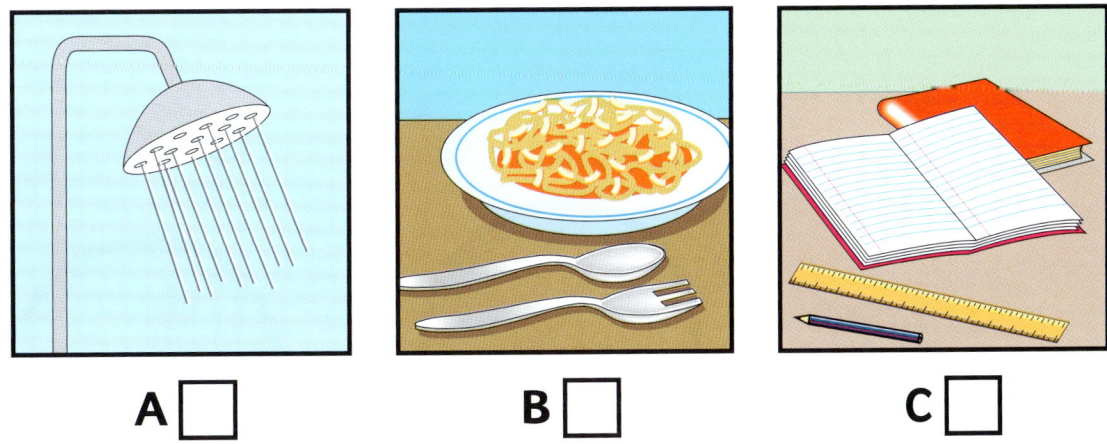

A ☐   B ☐   C ☐

Part 5
– 5 questions –

Listen and colour and write and draw. There is one example.

Reading and Writing

Part 1

– 10 questions –

Look and read. Choose the correct words and write them on the lines. There is one example.

a comic   a telephone   a restaurant   envelopes

You go over this to cross a road or a river. ....*a bridge*..........

rucksack

a farm

1   You put letters in these and write
    the addresses on the front of them.   ....

2   When you go on holiday you write
    on these and send them to your friends.
    They have pictures on them.   ....

3   You put things in this and carry it
    on your back.   ....

chemist's

a circus

4   In this competition everyone runs, and
    the person that finishes first wins.   ....

5   You write in this about things that have
    happened to you or things that you
    are going to do.   ....

6   You usually play this game outside
    in a team of eleven people and you
    wear shorts and a shirt.   ....

postcards

a diary

7   You can see clowns and animals like
    horses and elephants at this place.   ....

8   You can buy medicine, and sometimes
    brushes, combs and soap at this place.   ....

9   You can use this to talk to your
    friends and your family when you
    are not with them.   ....

football

golf

10 You can eat lunch or dinner at this
    place. Other people cook food for
    you and bring it to your table.   ....

a bridge   a torch   a race

Part 2
– 7 questions –

Look and read. Write yes or no.

Examples

The person who is skiing is
wearing a yellow hat.   *yes*

A pilot is flying a green
plane high in the sky.   *no*

Questions

1   Two boys are drinking hot chocolate under the trees.   ....

2   A girl with curly hair is skating across the lake.   ....

3   The small monster's skates are too big for its feet.   ....

4   The snowman's nose is made from a tomato and he's
    wearing a scarf with spots on it.   ....

5   The girl in the red jacket has put her foot through
    the ice.   ....

6   A boy is going down the hill on a sledge.   ....

7   One of the bigger monsters is throwing a snowball at
    another monster.   ....

Part 3
– 5 questions –

Read the text and choose the best answer.

Example

Harry: What are you doing, Jill?

Jill: A   You're reading a story.

                                                 B   He's doing his
                                                      homework.

                                                 Ⓒ   I'm looking for a book.

Questions

1   **Harry:**   Have you done your homework?

     Jill: A   Yes, I do.

                                                 B   Yes, I have.

                                                 C   Yes, I am.

2 **Harry:**   Can you help me with mine? It's very hard.

   Jill: A   I'll try.

                                          B   You can't.

                                          C   She did it.

3 **Harry:**   OK. This is the first question. Where does sugar come from?

   Jill: A   It lives in the jungle.

                                          B   I don't know.

                                          C   We have it with coffee and tea.

4 **Harry:**   Oh. How do you spell 'factory'?

   Jill: A   Let's look in the dictionary.

                                          B   You didn't spell it.

                                        C   My dad works in one.

5 **Woman:**   Can you be quiet please? I'm trying to read!.

   Jill: A   Yes, please.

                                          B   No, thank you.

                                          C   Oh, sorry.

Part 4
– 6 questions –

Read the story. Look at the pictures and the two examples.
Write one-word answers.

Jane's baby brother Tom is only eighteen months old. Jane has got a pet

.........................fish..................... called Sunny that lives in a bowl. One day, Tom put

his hands in the bowl and tried to catch Sunny. Of course, Jane was very

.........................unhappy..................... about this, so she decided to put Sunny's bowl on

the highest .... in the kitchen. 'Be careful!' said Jane's

dad when she was putting it up there. 'That's dangerous!' But Jane said,

'It's OK, Dad, Tom can't .... up there.' The next morning,

when Jane went downstairs she saw her cat in the kitchen.

He was playing with something .... 'Help, Dad!' she

shouted. 'The cat's got Sunny!' 'That's not Sunny,' said her dad. 'Look!

He's in his bowl. It's only a ....!' 'I'm going to move

Sunny's bowl again,' Jane said. 'The kitchen is too dangerous! Where can

I put it?' she asked. 'Put it in your .... ,' he answered,

'and don't let Tom or the cat go in there!'

What's the best name for this story?

Tick one box.

Sunny hurts a cat ☐

Tom's beautiful fish ☐

Sunny's new home ☐

Part 5
– 7 questions –

Look at the pictures and read the story. Answer the questions. Do not write more than *four* words in each answer.

Last weekend, Betty played with her friends Helen and Richard. First they played volleyball, then they went to the park and climbed trees. 'This is boring,' said Helen. 'I know a good game, but we need an umbrella.' They went to her house and found a big umbrella. Helen opened it and stood on a chair, then she jumped off. 'Look! I can fly!' she said. 'That chair isn't very high,' said Richard. 'Watch me!' He took the umbrella and jumped off a table.

Example

Who did Betty play with last weekend?   Helen and Richard

Questions

1   Where did they climb trees?   ....

2   What did Helen jump off?   ....

Betty wanted to fly too. 'I'm going to jump off the balcony!' she said. 'Stop!' shouted Richard. 'It's too high!' 'No, it isn't,' said Betty. They went upstairs to the balcony. Betty could see the garden below her, and it was a long way down. She was afraid, but she opened the umbrella and jumped. She fell into the flowers. Helen and Richard quickly ran downstairs. 'Betty, are you OK?' they asked. 'No! My leg hurts. I've broken it!' she answered.

3   Who jumped off the balcony?   ....

4   How did Betty feel when she looked
      down at the garden?   ....

5   Which part of her body did Betty hurt?   ....

When Helen told her mum, she took Betty to the hospital. A doctor looked at Betty's leg. 'You're OK, Betty. This time you haven't broken your leg, but don't try to fly again,' she said. The next day Betty's friends gave her a card. It said, 'Go by plane next time, Betty!'

6   Where did Helen's mum take Betty?   ....

7   What did Betty get from her friends?   ....

Blank Page

Part 6
– 10 questions –

Read the text. Choose the right words and write them on the lines.

ZOOS

Example Many people visit zoos .... *every* .... year. They go to zoos

1 .... they enjoy seeing animals and learning more

2 about them. Animals from many different parts ....

the world live there. You can usually see lions, tigers, elephants,

camels and monkeys, and also fish, frogs and snakes. You can draw

3 the animals or take photos of .... , and in some

zoos you can watch videos too. Sometimes you can ride elephants or

4 camels. The people .... give the animals food have

5 to work very .... Every day they give them food

6 and water and clean .... homes. Some animals eat

7 leaves, fruit and vegetables, ... others eat meat or

8 fish. At London Zoo .... are also pets, like mice and

rabbits, and farm animals, like sheep and goats. Children can play

9 with .... animals. Most animals are beautiful, but

10 some of them can .... dangerous.

Example	any	every	some
1	because	so	when
2	to	on	of
3	us	it	them
4	who	whose	which
5	hard	harder	hardest
6	its	their	your
7	or	but	if
8	they	there	here
9	these	this	that
10	be	being	been

Part 7
– 5 questions –

Read the diary and write the missing words. Write one word on each line.

	Sunday
Example	Something horrible happened to me yesterday! ....In.................
1	the afternoon I went to Sue's house. 'Would you ....
2	a cup of tea?' she asked me. 'Yes, please,' ....
	answered. She went to the kitchen and made the tea.
3	'................................. you take sugar?' she shouted from there. 'Yes,
	three spoons of sugar for me!' I said. Then she brought me the tea.
	When I drank it, it tasted very strange. 'Sue, you've
4	.... salt in my tea, not sugar!' I said. 'Oh, no!' said
5	Sue. 'I .... sorry!'

Blank Page

Part 1
– 5 questions –

Listen and draw lines. There is one example.

Michael Sarah Harry Katy Helen Richard William

Part 2
– 5 questions –

Listen and write. There is one example.

	Name:	.... Mr Powers ....
1	Job:	....
2	Works at:	.... Airport
3	How he goes to work:	....
4	Starts work at:	.... on Saturdays
5	Favourite sport:	....

Part 3

– 5 questions –

Which animal pictures has Sally got on her things?

Listen and write letters in the boxes. There is one example.

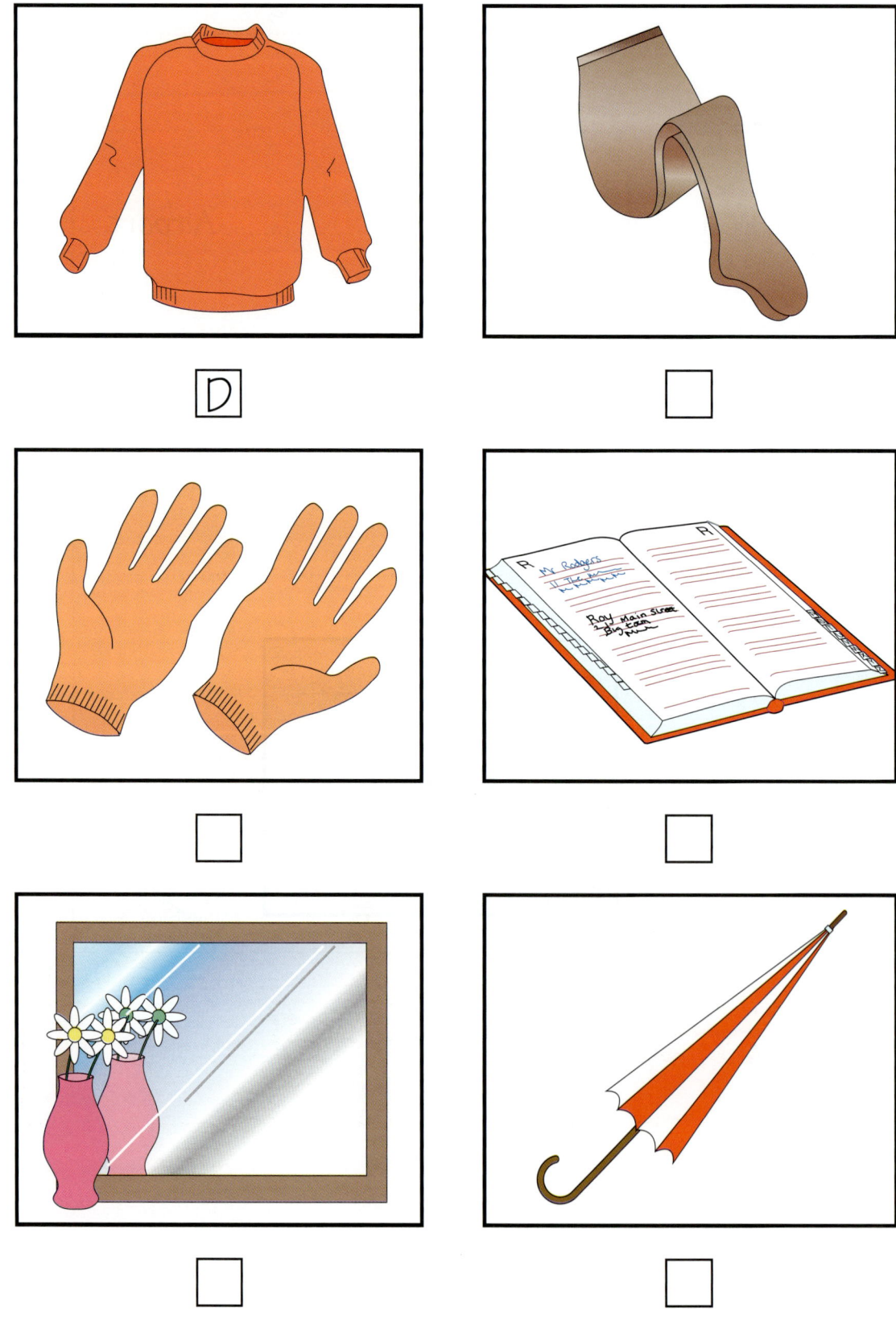

A

B

C

D

E

F

G

H

Part 4
– 5 questions –

Listen and tick (✔) the box. There is one example.

Where did Sarah go for her birthday?

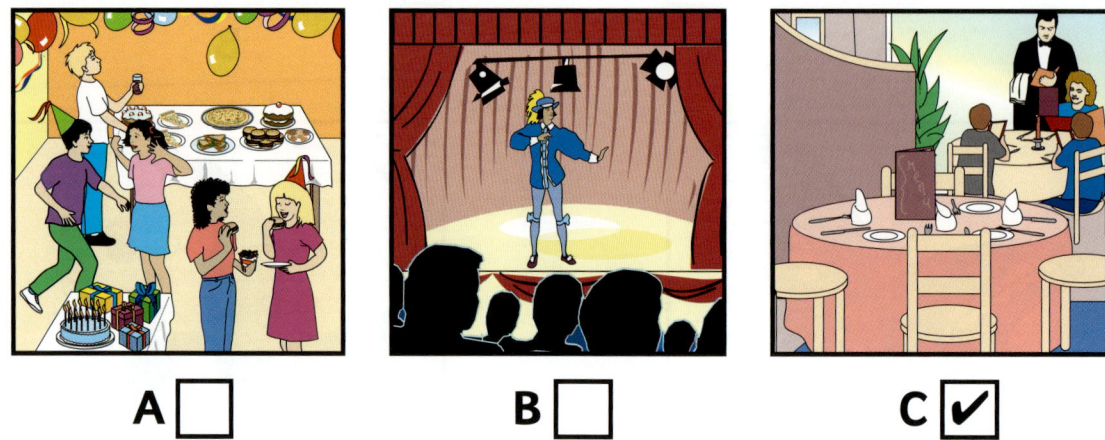

A ☐   B ☐   C ✔

1   Who went with Sarah?

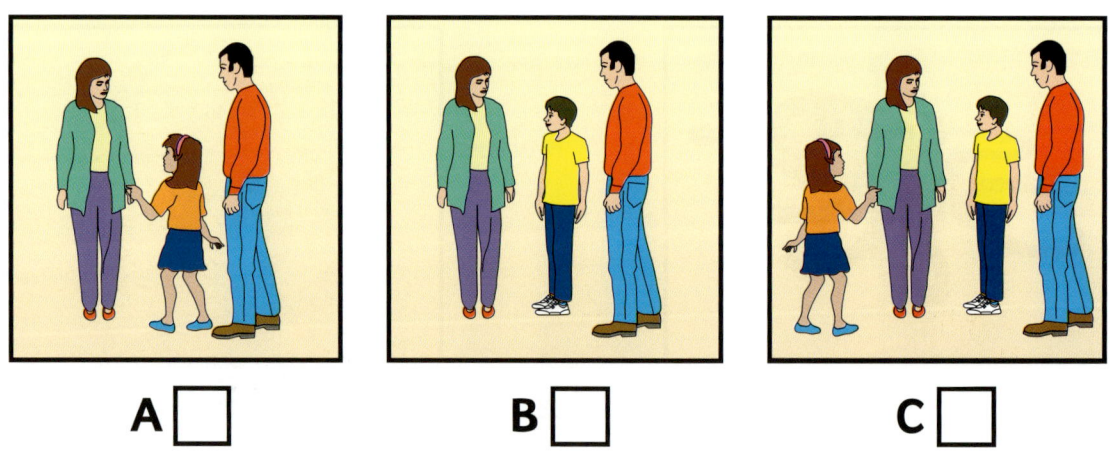

A ☐   B ☐   C ☐

2   Which is Sarah's favourite present?

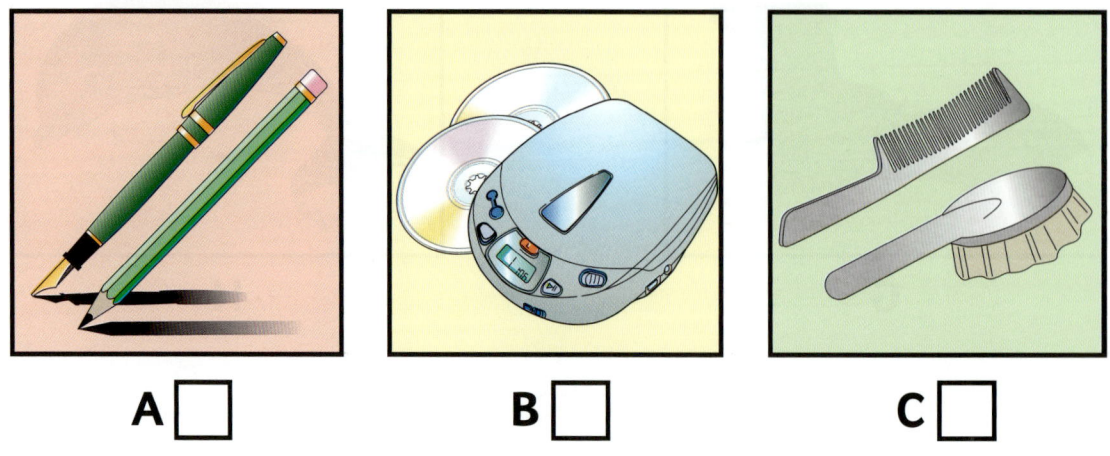

A ☐   B ☐   C ☐

3   What does Sarah like most at the circus?

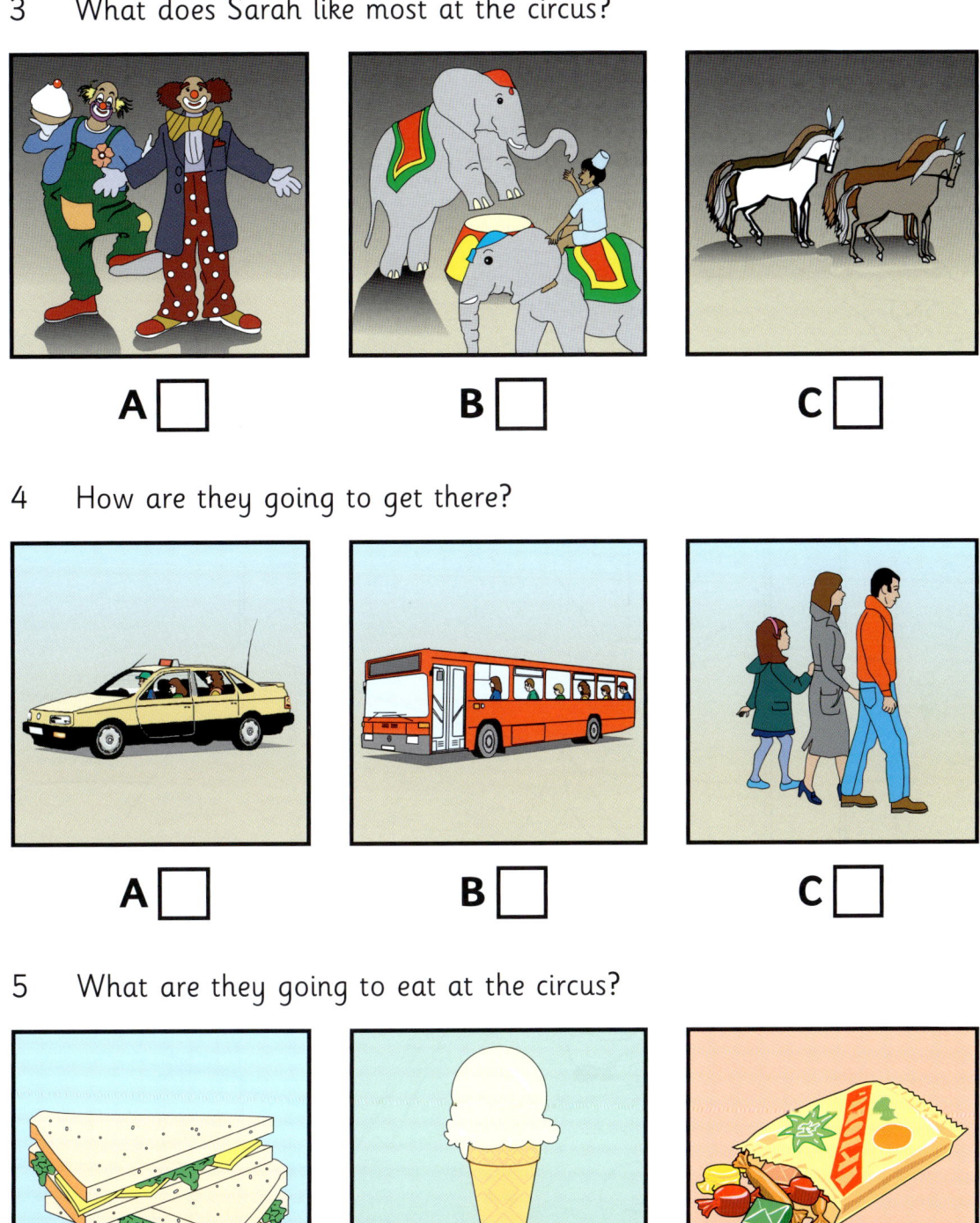

A ☐   B ☐   C ☐

4   How are they going to get there?

A ☐   B ☐   C ☐

5   What are they going to eat at the circus?

A ☐   B ☐   C ☐

Part 5
– 5 questions –

Listen and colour and write and draw. There is one example.

Reading and Writing

Part 1
– 10 questions –

Look and read. Choose the correct words and write them on the lines. There is one example.

wool   a snack   clouds   wood

a camel   salt

	Some people who live in hot, dry countries may ride on this animal.	*a camel*
1	This little animal has eight legs and it catches flies and eats them.	....
2	When people cook, they often put this in the food. It is white and you can get it from the sea.	....
3	This comes from trees, and tables and chairs are often made from it.	....
4	Before it rains, you see a lot of these in the sky. They are white or grey.	....
5	This is usually made from fruit and you can eat it with bread.	....
6	Breakfast, lunch and dinner are all examples of these.	....
7	Windows are usually made of this. It is hard, but easy to break.	....
8	You can skate on this or put a piece of it in a cold drink.	....
9	You sometimes see these in the sky after it rains. They have seven colours in them.	....
10	There is a lot of this in cakes, chocolate, ice cream and sweets.	....

a spider   glass

meals   ice

jam   a lizard

rainbows   sugar   storms

Part 2
– 7 questions –

Look and read. Write yes or no.

Examples

The girl is wearing red tights with
yellow spots on them.

......................yes......................

The boy on the swing has got short
black hair.

......................no......................

Questions

1   One of the boy's socks is falling into the grass.   ....

2   Some clothes are in the tree because it is very windy.   ....

3   The bicycle under the tree has two flags on it.   ....

4   The girl is carrying a bowl which is full of fruit.   ....

5   There is only one apple on the tree now.   ....

6   One of the rabbits has picked up a leaf.   ....

7   The biggest cloud in the sky is the grey one.   ....

Part 3
– 5 questions –

Read the text and choose the best answer.

Example

Harry: Hello Sarah. When did you get home from your holiday?

Sarah: A   Next Tuesday.

ⓑ   Two days ago.

C   A few days before.

Questions

1   **Harry:**   How was your holiday?

Sarah: A   It's great!

B   Excellent!

C   Very well!

2 **Harry:**   Where did you go?

   Sarah: A   We visited my uncle's
                                                      farm.

                                                 B   We're going to the
                                                      mountains.

                                                 C   We took the train there.

3 **Harry:**   You go there every year. Doesn't it get boring?

   Sarah: A   No. We are never
                                                      boring.

                                                 B   Oh, no! There's always
                                                      something new to do.

                                                 C   No. You don't like going
                                                      there.

4 **Harry:**   What was the most interesting thing that you did?

   Sarah: A   It's more interesting
                                                      than the strange cave
                                                      paintings.

                                                 B   I'd like to see those
                                                      strange paintings in
                                                      a cave.

                                                 C   We went to see some
                                                      strange paintings in
                                                      a cave.

5 **Harry:**   Did you get any good photos?

   Sarah: A   Yes, you got some
                                                      interesting ones.

                                                 B   Yes, you must come
                                                      and see them.

                                                 C   Yes, they're too dark.

Part 4
– 6 questions –

**Read the story. Look at the pictures and the two examples.
Write one-word answers.**

Katy and her family moved to a new house on a hot and

........sunny........ day last week. Katy put her toys into her

........rucksack........ . It wasn't very big so she couldn't take all her old

toys. She took only the toys that she still played with – her video games,

drum, beach ball, kite and her favourite dolls. She threw her old and dirty

toys in the .... Then she put all her school things in her

school bag and took it .... Everyone in the family

had to .... some boxes, bags and suitcases. Katy was

ready to leave, but she couldn't find her cat, Charlie. He wasn't in the

house because it was too .... for him. Katy went into the

street and called 'Charlie!' She couldn't see him, but then she heard crying

near the car. She .... the door, and there he was.

What's the best name for this story?

Tick one box.

Katy loses her favourite toy ☐

Where is Charlie? ☐

Katy's new pet ☐

Part 5
– 7 questions –

**Look at the pictures and read the story. Answer the questions.
Do not write more than *four* words in each answer.**

Last Sunday morning, Ann and her brother Ben tidied the living room. Their little brother Harry tried to help too. Everything had to be ready for the party before Emma arrived. The party was a secret that Emma didn't know about. It was her twelfth birthday. Emma has never had a birthday party before. Her parents usually take her to a restaurant for dinner on her birthday.

Example

When did the children tidy the living room?   *last Sunday morning*

Questions

1   How old is Emma now?   ....

2   Who didn't know about the party?   ....

3   Where does Emma usually go on
    her birthday?   ....

When Emma arrived, Ann and Ben shouted 'Happy Birthday!' 'What's happening?' said Emma. 'We're having a party for you!' they said. 'Great!' Emma said. Then Ann pointed to a table in the corner of the living room, and said 'Look at this!' On the table was a birthday cake. It was a big, chocolate cake. 'It looks lovely,' said Emma. 'Let's have some now.' Emma had a big piece first, then cut two big pieces for Ann and Ben. She only gave a small piece to Harry because he is still a baby.

4   What kind of cake did they have?   ....

5   Who had the smallest piece of cake?   ....

Then Emma opened her presents, and after that they put some music on, and started dancing. Suddenly, Ann stopped. 'Where's Harry?' she said. The other children stopped dancing and looked, and then they saw baby Harry. He was on the table, eating chocolate cake! There was chocolate cake on his face, hands, clothes and on the floor! 'Oh no! Stop it, Harry!' Ann shouted. But Harry only said, 'Cake, cake, cake!' 'He likes Emma's cake, I think!' Ben said, and they all laughed.

6   Who stopped dancing first?   ....

7   Where was baby Harry?   ....

Blank Page

Part 6
– 10 questions –

Read the text. Choose the right words and write them on the lines.

SHARKS

Example   Most people are afraid of sharks but ....*some*.................. sharks are

not dangerous. There are many different kinds of shark. All sharks

1   eat fish and a few .... eat plants. The whale shark

2   is the biggest shark in the world .... it eats only the

smallest fish and plants.

3   Sharks .... live in hot or cold water and they

4   never .... swimming – they sleep and swim at the

5   same time! They swim very fast and they look ....

6   food in big groups. They can't see very .... so they

use their noses to find food. If a shark is very hungry, it will eat

7   any fish that swims .... Sometimes one shark will

8   start eating .... shark that gets in

9   .... way.

10   Only a few kinds of sharks eat people, and this ....

not happen very often. We should remember that the sharks in films

are very different from the sharks that live in our seas!

Example	any	some	every
1	still	also	too
2	so	but	if
3	should	can	need
4	stop	stopped	stopping
5	to	after	for
6	well	good	better
7	across	past	before
8	others	other	another
9	its	their	a
10	has	does	is

Part 7
– 5 questions –

Read the postcard and write the missing words. Write one word on each line.

Dear Daisy,

Example I can't believe that we've ....*been*.......... here for a week

1 already. This city is very interesting and ....

are a lot of things to see. We've visited art museums, churches,

castles and we've seen the lions and tigers at the city's famous

2 ....

3 We went to the theatre .... night and we saw one of

our favourite actors! The food is our only problem here. It's too

4 expensive .... eat in restaurants and the food in cheap

cafés isn't very good. I will be very hungry next Tuesday night, when I

5 come to .... house for supper! See you then.

Love, Sara

Blank Page

Examiner's copy

Find the difference

Candidate's copy

Find the difference

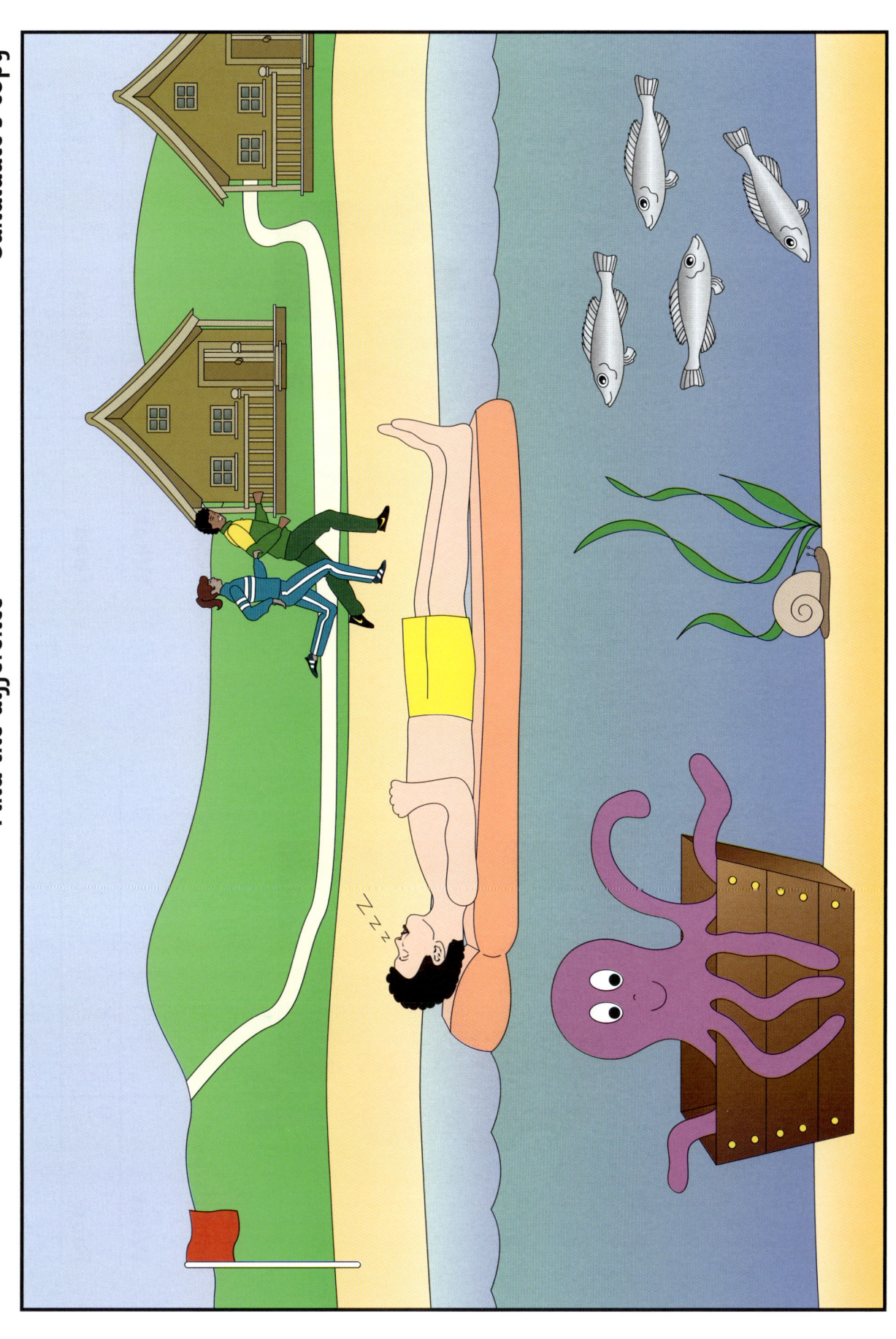

Examiner's copy

Peter's pet

What	frog
Food	spiders
Colour	green and brown
How old	8 months
Name	Fred

Information exchange

Mary's pet

What	?
Food	?
Colour	?
How old	?
Name	?

Candidate's copy

Peter's pet

What	?
Food	?
Colour	?
How old	?
Name	?

Information exchange

Mary's pet

What	horse
Food	carrots
Colour	brown and black
How old	6 years old
Name	Harry

Tell the story

Blank Page

Find the difference

Candidate's copy

Find the difference

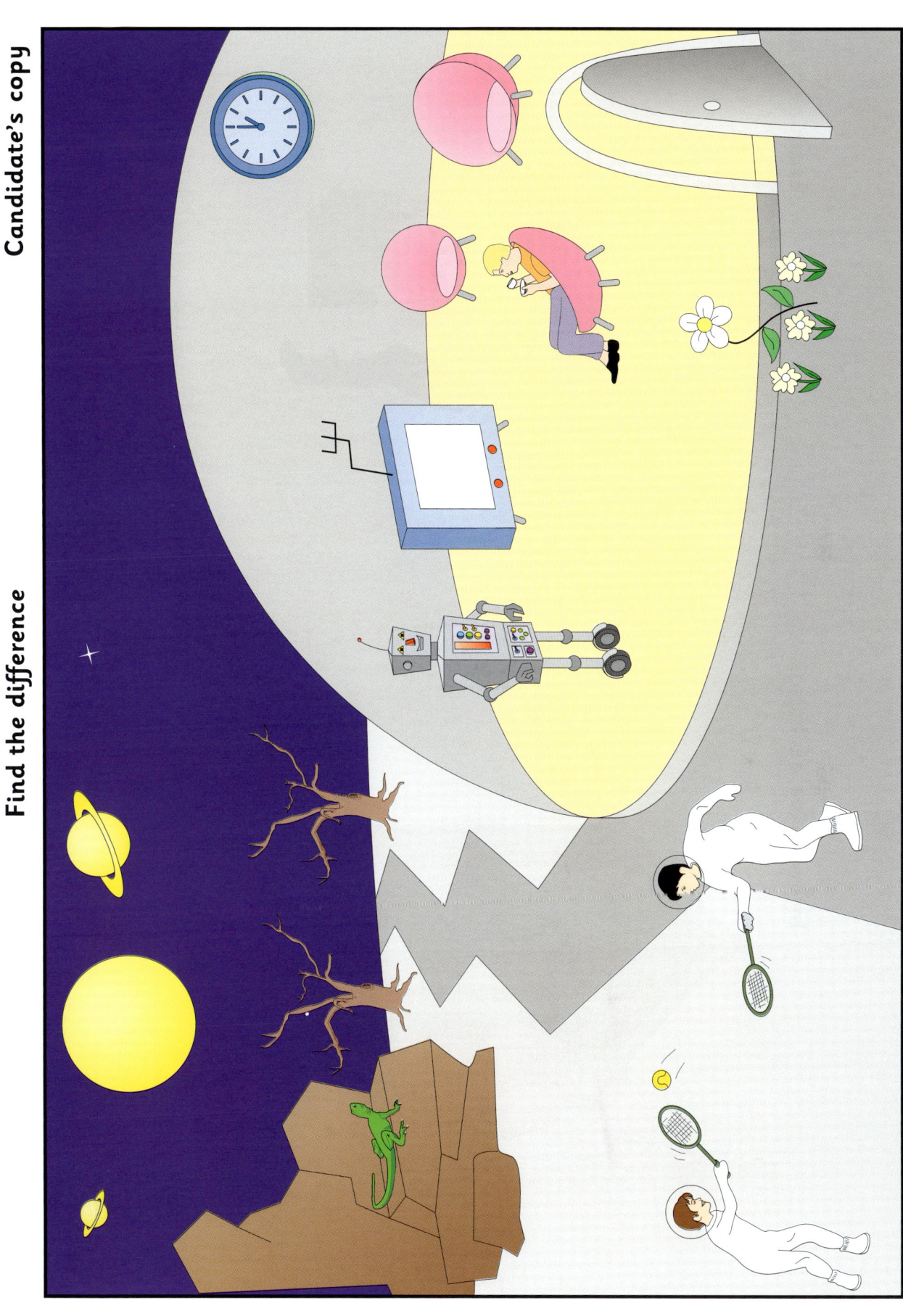

Examiner's copy

What	frog
Food	spiders
Colour	green and brown
How old	8 months
Name	Fred

Information exchange

What	?
Food	?
Colour	?
How old	?
Name	?

Candidate's copy

Peter's pet

What	?
Food	?
Colour	?
How old	?
Name	?

Information exchange

Mary's pet

What	horse
Food	carrots
Colour	brown and b.ack
How old	6 years old
Name	Harry

Tell the story

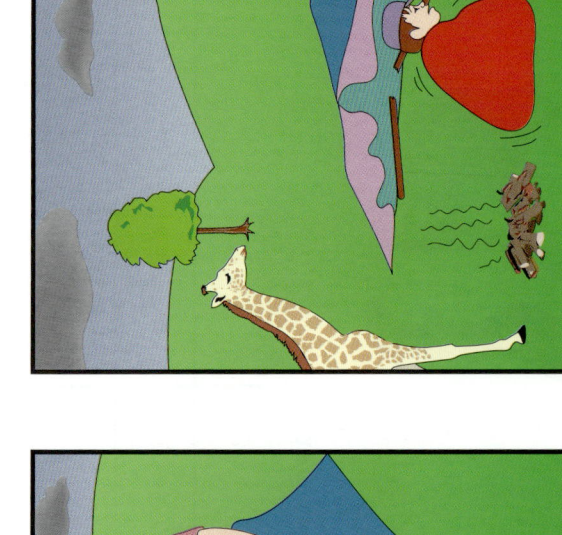

Speaking

Candidate's copy

Find the difference

Examiner's copy

Information exchange

Peter's bedroom

Upstairs/downstairs	downstairs
Next to	kitchen
Colour/walls	red
How many windows	three
Favourite thing	television

Paul's bedroom

Upstairs/downstairs	?
Next to	?
Colour/walls	?
How many windows	?
Favourite thing	?

Candidate's copy

Information exchange

Paul's bedroom

Upstairs/downstairs	upstairs
Next to	bathroom
Colour/walls	blue
How many windows	two
Favourite thing	computer

Peter's bedroom

Upstairs/downstairs	?
Next to	?
Colour/walls	?
How many windows	?
Favourite thing	?

Tell the story

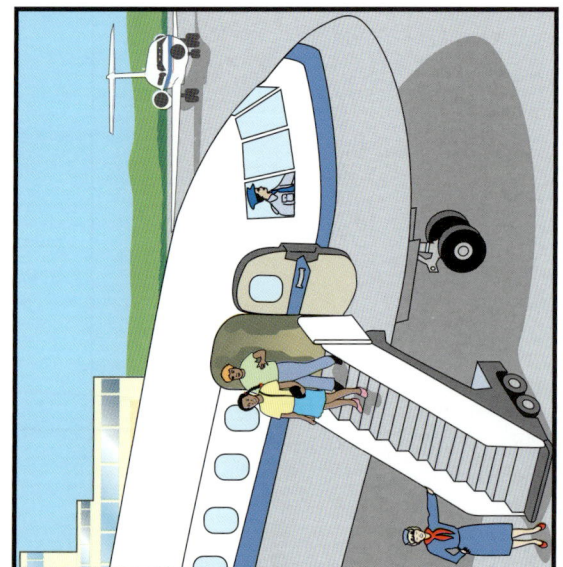

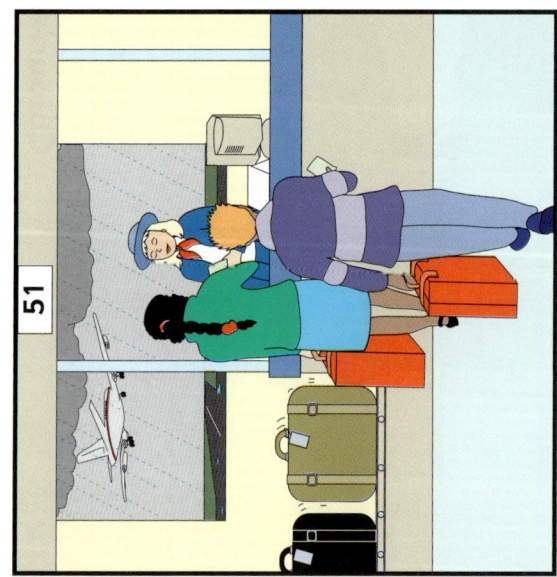

51

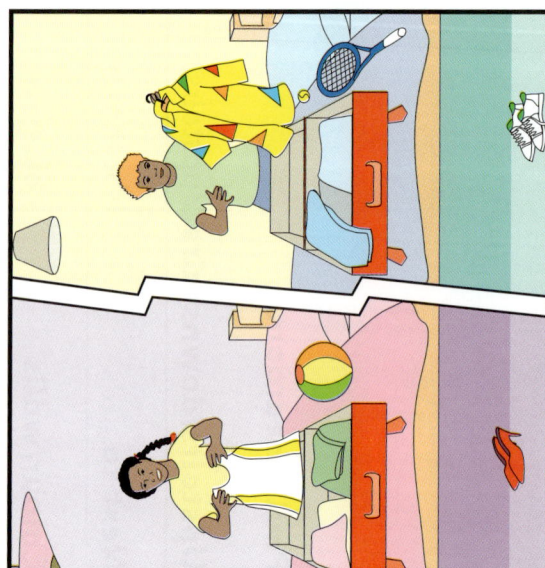

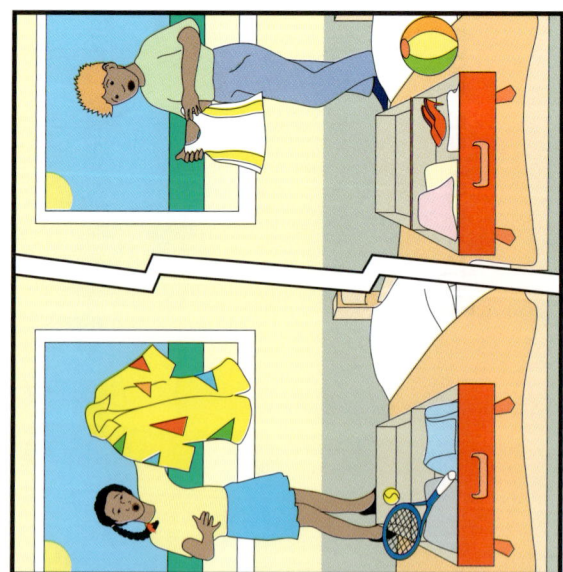